better together*

*This book is best read together, grownup and kid.

a kids
book
about

a kids book about

POWER

by Juliyen Davis

A Kids Co.
Editors Denise Morales Soto & Jennifer Goldstein
Designer Jelani Memory
Creative Director Rick DeLucco
Studio Manager Kenya Feldes
Sales Director Melanie Wilkins
Head of Books Jennifer Goldstein
CEO and Founder Jelani Memory

DK
Senior Production Editor Jennifer Murray
Senior Production Controller Louise Minihane
Senior Acquisitions Editor Katy Flint
Acquisitions Project Editor Sara Forster
Managing Art Editor Vicky Short
Managing Director, Licensing Mark Searle

First American edition, 2025
Published in the United States by DK Publishing, 1745 Broadway, 20th Floor,
New York, NY 10019

First published in Great Britain in 2025 by
Dorling Kindersley Limited, 20 Vauxhall Bridge Road, London SW1V 2SA
A Penguin Random House Company

The authorised representative in the EEA is
Dorling Kindersley Verlag GmbH. Arnulfstr. 124, 80636 Munich, Germany

A catalog record for this book is available from the Library of Congress.
A CIP catalogue record for this book is available from the British Library.
ISBN: 978-0-2417-4308-9

DK books are available at special discounts when purchased in bulk for sales
promotions, premiums, fund-raising, or education use. For details, contact:
DK Publishing Special Markets, 1745 Broadway, 20th Floor, New York, NY 10019
SpecialSales@dk.com

Printed and bound in China
www.dk.com
akidsco.com

MIX
Paper | Supporting
responsible forestry
FSC™ C018179

This book was made with Forest
Stewardship Council™ certified
paper – one small step in DK's
commitment to a sustainable future.
Learn more at **www.dk.com/uk/
information/sustainability**

For us.

Intro
for grownups

It's easy to feel powerless in the face of bullying, depression, racism, addiction, and other adversities, but it's important to remember that no person, place, or thing has power without us. Despite the classic stories portraying power as something that only a few special people have, the real power is within all of us as soon as we feel empowered to recognize it.

Reading this book, I hope you begin to recognize both the small and big ways that power influences the world around us, and I hope you feel more empowered to see how you, specifically, can influence it positively.

Hey, there!

I want to ask you something.

DO YOU FEEL POWER

You don't have

FUL?

to answer that yet. We'll come back to it.

Let me ask you something else.

When you hear the word power, **what do you think of?**

Do you think of flexing your **muscles**?

Do you think of your favorite **superhero**?

What if I told you that power could be as simple as...

WORDS?

You see,
power isn't just one thing,
or person, or place.

It's also not some magical thing that's far beyond our reach and only a special few have.

Power,

at its core, is how one thing, person, or place influences* another thing, person, or place.

*Influence means when a person or thing affects someone or something in an important way.

Confused?

THAT'S OK!

Power is **REALLY** complicated and difficult to understand.

Even for grownups!

But I'm going to try my best to explain it to you.

Think of your teacher...

or your doctor,

or your parents.

They all have power because they influence those around them...

in the classroom,

at the hospital,

and at home.

They are influenced by the people, things, and places around them as well, maybe in smaller ways...

we just don't see.

We interact with power every day—
even when we don't know it!

Some might use their power to

HURT
PEOPLE

or make them

FEEL
SMALL.

Others use their power to inspire and stick up for others.

POWER IS NOT GOOD OR BAD OR BIG OR SMALL BY ITSELF.

The person who makes that call is, well, **YOU.**

Power is what

make it.

It couldn't exist without you.

We all have power and the ability to influence and affect those around us.

Maybe that's in teeny-tiny ways you don't even notice, like listening and talking about new ideas which you discover.

Or in **REALLY** big ways that everybody can see,

like starting a fundraiser
or defending someone who is
being treated badly.

ONE, SINGLE PERSON HAS THE POWER TO DO GREAT THINGS.

Even when they don't think they can.

Remember all of those powerful folks we talked about earlier in this book?

They don't just have that power—we give it to them.

You, me, and everybody around us.

And the more power we give to them, **the bigger the effect of their actions.**

We can choose to grow the
power of those who help us...

POWER POWE
POWER POWE
POWER POWE
POWER POWE
POWER POWE
POWER

and we can also take power back
from the people who hurt us.

We can do that by using our words.

By thinking about our actions.

And by recognizing the influence we have on those around us.

You don't have to do it alone!

BECAUSE GUESS WHAT?

adds up!

When we combine our **words**...

and our **actions**...

and all of our **individual power**...

WE **CAN** MAKE

CHANGE.

We are all capable of doing great things and helping each other once we learn to see power and the role it plays in our lives.

Where do you see power in your **life**?

What influence does it have on **you**?

What effect does it have on **others**?

How are **YOU** empowering others?

And in those moments of doubt,
I dare you to ask yourself again...

DO YOU FEEL ERFUL?

Outro
for grownups

Now that you've made it to the end of the book, you and your kiddo may have some questions. Why does it feel like some people have more power than I do? What power do I have? How do I know if I'm having a positive influence on those around me when I use my power? Is it only people that can have power—what about technology or nature? How is power distributed, and is it really as simple as give-and-take? What's the difference between power and privilege?

You may not have all of the answers, but that's OK! Power doesn't have an easy answer, definition, or response. Take advantage of this opportunity to reflect and learn alongside your kid. This book is meant to be the beginning of a long series of conversations about power. Be vigilant and observant about where power shows up in your life and use examples from your experience when questions come up. It's important to be honest and talk about the power you have and how you use it.

About The Author

Juliyen Davis (he/him) grew up in a small town—a town mostly known for its paper mill. Always one of a few people of color growing up, it would have been easy for him to feel small...but instead, he learned to feel empowered.

He went to college to study economics and worked in investment, philanthropy, and city government. With this experience, he continued to Parsons and pivoted his focus to transdisciplinary design and creative technology.

Despite inequality, racism, climate change, war—all that the world may throw at us—we can learn to see the power we hold within ourselves, and choose: to power together, to power through, and to make powerful change. That is what this book is about...from Juliyen, to you.

@juliyennnnnnnnnnnn   in @juliyendavis

Made to empower.

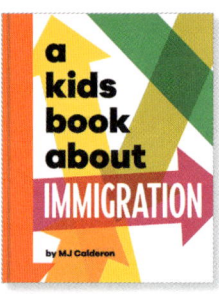
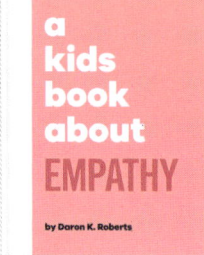
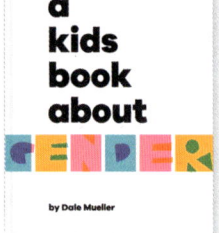
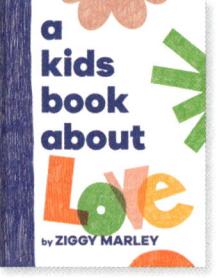
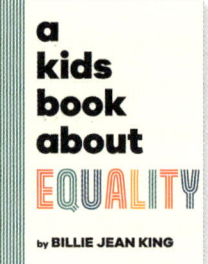

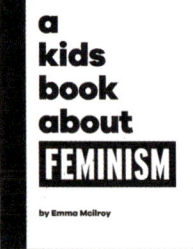
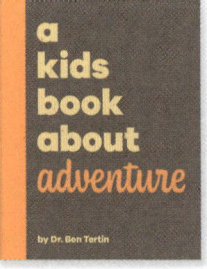

Discover more at akidsco.com